COUNTDOWN TO SPACE

JOHN GLENN
A Space Biography

Barbara Kramer

Series Advisor:
John E. McLeaish
Chief, Public Information Office, retired,
NASA Johnson Space Center

Enslow Publishers, Inc.

44 Fadem Road	PO Box 38
Box 699	Aldershot
Springfield, NJ 07081	Hants GU12 6BP
USA	UK

Library of Congress Cataloging-in-Publication Data

Kramer, Barbara
    John Glenn: a space biography / Barbara Kramer.
        p. cm. — (Countdown to space)
    Includes bibliographical references and index.
    Summary: A biography of the first American to orbit the Earth, covering his
youth, his career as an astronaut, and his life after NASA.
    ISBN 0-89490-964-9
    1. Glenn, John, 1921–   —Juvenile literature. 2. Astronauts—United States—
Biography—Juvenile literature. [1. Glenn, John, 1921–   . 2. Astronauts.
3. Legislators.] I. Title. II. Series.
TL789.85.G6K73 1998
629.45'0092—dc21
[B]   97-17978
                                                    CIP
                                                       AC

Printed in the United States of America

10 9 8 7 6 5 4 3 2 1

Illustration Credits: Library of Congress, p. 14; National Aeronautics and
Space Administration (NASA), pp. 6, 8, 11, 15, 22, 24, 25, 27, 29, 39;
National Archives, pp. 4, 18, 20, 35, 37.

Cover Illustration: National Aeronautics and Space Administration
(NASA) (foreground); Raghvendra Sahai and John Trauger (JPL), the
WFPC2 science team, NASA, and AURA/STSCI (background).

CONTENTS

John Glenn looks to be in great spirits as he leaves the hangar prior to his Earth-orbiting flight on February 20, 1962.

A View from Space

On launchpad 14 in Cape Canaveral, Florida, a towering Atlas rocket stretched seventy feet into the air. Its shiny silver sides gleamed in the morning sun. On top of the rocket sat the small Mercury space capsule, *Friendship 7*. Inside the capsule, astronaut John Glenn waited. It was February 20, 1962. In a few minutes, he would be blasted into space.

Two other astronauts, Alan B. Shepard, Jr., and Virgil I. Grissom, had been launched from this same spot. Shepard had flown on May 5, 1961, and Grissom on July 21, 1961. Their flights were called suborbital flights because they did not orbit, or travel around, Earth.

They had shot off the launchpad and into space on top of Redstone rockets. However, once they reached

space, the capsules made a turnaround and headed back to Earth, where they splashed down in the Atlantic Ocean. The flights took only about fifteen minutes each.

Launching a man into space was an important step in space exploration, but now it was time to go one step farther. Today, John Glenn would become the first American to attempt to orbit Earth.

The Redstone rocket that Shepard and Grissom had used was dependable, but it did not have enough power to actually get a space capsule into orbit. For that, the larger, more powerful Atlas rocket was needed. Unfortunately, it was not as dependable.

Towering high above the ground, the Friendship 7 *capsule sat on the Atlas rocket, waiting for John Glenn to ride it into space.*

In previous unmanned flights, the Atlas rocket had exploded shortly after leaving the launchpad. Changes had been made to make the rocket safer, but no one could be certain that it would perform without a problem today. Glenn would be the first astronaut to be launched into space by the Atlas rocket. He knew he was risking his life. On the other hand, he had confidence in the space program and everyone who had worked to get this far. It was a risk he was willing to take.

Glenn was lying on his back inside the capsule. He was strapped to a couch that had been specially made to fit his five-foot eleven-inch frame. Earlier, the bright red gantry, or service tower, had been rolled away from the rocket. Without the support of the gantry, the rocket swayed with each gust of wind.

At T minus thirty-five seconds, the umbilical cord that supplied power to the capsule dropped away. It was the last link between the capsule and the ground.

Excitement was building in the control center. Glenn was feeling it too. The final seconds were ticking away.

Backup pilot Scott Carpenter radioed one final message to his friend. "Godspeed, John Glenn," he called.[1]

"Three seconds . . . two . . . one . . . zero!"[2]

Glenn felt the space capsule shake as the rocket's engines roared. Smoke billowed up around the capsule. For a couple of seconds, the rocket stayed on the launchpad as the engines built up power. Then it shot upward, rising on a white-yellow flame. It was 9:47 A.M.

Thirteen seconds after liftoff, Glenn reported on the flight so far. "Little bumpy along about here," he said.[3] The vibrations of the capsule caused his voice to tremble.

Glenn felt a weight squeezing his chest. It was the increase in g-forces caused by the acceleration of the vehicle. At one point, it was almost eight times stronger

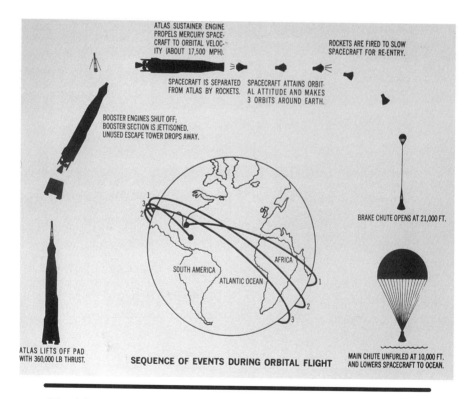

After lifting off the pad, the Atlas rocket would propel Friendship 7, *with John Glenn inside, into orbit around Earth.* Friendship 7 *would splash down into the Atlantic Ocean after its mission.*

than the pull of Earth's gravity. It pressed Glenn tight against the couch.

About two minutes into the flight, two of the three main engines on the Atlas rocket cut off, as planned. They had used up all their fuel. Glenn saw a cloud of smoke go by his window as the engines dropped away from the rocket.

The third engine boosted the capsule into orbit. Then it cut off as well. Glenn heard a loud bang as the clamps that held the Atlas rocket to the capsule released. The rocket was jettisoned into space. Now, there was only the Mercury capsule, with John Glenn sitting alone inside.

"Zero-g, and I feel fine," Glenn reported.[4] He was experiencing the weightlessness of space.

The capsule made a 180-degree turn, and Glenn looked down at Earth. "Oh, that view is tremendous!" he said.[5] He was now flying backward, zooming through space at over 17,500 miles per hour. He was in orbit— exciting news for everyone, including John Glenn. He had spent three years as an astronaut preparing for this flight, but his interest in flying had begun much sooner.

2

A Taste of Flying

John Herschel Glenn, Jr., came into the world on July 18, 1921. He was the only son of Clara and John Herschel Glenn, Sr. A few years later, his parents adopted a daughter, Jean.

Although John was named after his father, he was never called Junior. Instead, he went by the nickname Bud.

John lived in Cambridge, Ohio, for the first two years of his life. Then the family moved down the road a few miles to New Concord, Ohio. John's father started his own business there—Glenn's Heating and Plumbing.

New Concord was a small town where things like patriotism mattered. "There were certain things that everyone was absolutely expected to do," Glenn later said, "like saluting the flag and showing up at the graveyard with flowers on Memorial Day."[1]

Religion was also important. Many of the people in town were Presbyterians. They had strict religious beliefs. Smoking was not allowed. Alcoholic beverages were not sold anywhere in town.

John adopted those same beliefs. Patriotism and good clean living became a way of life for him. They were as much a part of him as his green eyes, red hair, and freckles.

On summer days in New Concord, John and his friends went swimming in Crooked Creek or played softball. In the winter, they went sledding or ice-skating.

John was interested in airplanes, although as a child, he never thought about actually piloting one through the skies. He was more interested in what made them fly and how they were put together.[2]

Once, a case of scarlet fever kept him home for a

As a young boy, John Glenn enjoyed swimming, softball, and sledding. He also developed a keen interest in airplanes.

couple of weeks. He spent that time in his room building model airplanes.

John wanted to be a Boy Scout, but there was no troop in his town. When he was twelve years old, he and some of his friends organized their own group, called the Ohio Rangers. "We told one another we were tougher than Scouts—so tough they wouldn't have us," one of the Rangers recalled. "We went in for endurance stuff—sleeping in sleet and rain, hiking in knee-deep snow, climbing eight-foot maples, swimming upstream."[3]

One of John's best friends was Annie Castor. They met when John was three years old and Annie was four. Their parents belonged to a small group of people who got together once a week for potluck dinner. Their children were always included, and it was at one of those dinners that John and Annie first met.

Annie was very outgoing, even though she spoke with an obvious stutter. It was hard for her to get her words out, but John never seemed to mind. "I never knew Annie at a time she did not stutter," he said.[4]

John attended New Concord High School. He was an honor student and played trumpet in the school band. He was active in sports, but he was not a natural athlete. He made up for his lack of athletic ability with determination. He became the only one in his high-school class to letter in three sports—football, basketball, and tennis. He was also a swimmer and worked as a lifeguard at a summer camp.

John's father had started another business—a car dealership. For John's sixteenth birthday, his father gave him a car off the lot. It was a 1929 Chevy Roadster with a canvas top. John painted it red and nicknamed it "The Cruiser." He almost always rode with the top down as he taxied his friends around town.

Annie Castor was a frequent passenger in "The Cruiser." By the time they were teenagers, their friends were used to seeing the two of them together. John never appeared to be interested in dating anyone else.

John graduated from high school in 1939. He then enrolled at Muskingum College, a small Presbyterian school in New Concord. His major was chemical engineering. Annie Castor was also a student there. She majored in music.

During his second year of college, Glenn enrolled in a Navy program for civilians and learned how to fly. "I was sold on flying as soon as I had a taste of it," he later wrote.[5] He received his private pilot's license on July 1, 1941.

Five months later, on December 7, the Japanese bombed Pearl Harbor, Hawaii. That incident drew the United States into World War II. Glenn left school to join the Navy.

He earned his wings in Corpus Christi, Texas, on March 31, 1943. He had achieved the rank of second

John Glenn lounges in front of a group of fellow ice-skaters. Seated behind Glenn, second from the right, is his smiling wife, Annie.

lieutenant. Because of his high scores during training, Glenn was given a choice. He could stay in the Navy or join the Marine Corps. Glenn decided to become a Marine.

He made a quick trip back to New Concord, Ohio, to marry Annie Castor on April 6. He soon received his orders for overseas duty. By that time, he had been promoted to the rank of first lieutenant.

Glenn flew fifty-nine air-to-ground missions in the Marshall Islands. This group of islands in the Pacific Ocean were occupied by Japan. Glenn's efforts in the war earned him two Distinguished Flying Crosses and ten Air Medals.

After a year of combat duty, Glenn was sent back to the United States. He was stationed at the Patuxent Naval Air Station in Maryland. In July 1945, he was promoted to captain. The war ended on September 2. Three months later, on December 13, his son, David, was born.

After the war, Glenn decided to stay on as a Marine. In 1947, he was assigned to his second tour of overseas duty. He was flying patrol over North China when his daughter, Carolyn (Lyn), was born on March 19, 1947. Three years later, the United States was once again at war, this time with North Korea.

A 1961 photograph shows John Glenn's family—daughter Lyn, 14; son David, 16; and wife, Annie.

3

"Ol' Magnet Tail"

Glenn was a flight instructor at Corpus Christi, Texas, when the Korean War began. Korea was a country situated on a small peninsula along northeastern China. After World War II, it had been divided into two countries—North and South Korea. In 1950, troops from North Korea invaded South Korea. The United States helped the South Koreans defend their country.

Glenn was sent back to combat duty in 1953 and was assigned to fly air-to-ground missions over Korea. He was determined to do a good job. Glenn did not like to pull out of bombing dives until his target had been completely destroyed. As a result, he often got hit by enemy fire. "We called Glenn ol' magnet tail because his plane was hit so many times in combat," one pilot joked.[1]

Later, Glenn got a chance to fly in air-to-air combat. His job then was to chase down enemy MiG planes. In one nine-day period, he shot down three MiGs. That was just before the war ended on July 27, 1953.

Glenn flew a total of ninety missions during the Korean War. He earned his third and fourth Distinguished Flying Crosses and was awarded eight more Air Medals.

For a young pilot used to excitement, the next step was to become a test pilot. Glenn was accepted at the Naval Test Pilot School at the Patuxent Naval Air Station in Maryland. He knew that he had some hard work ahead of him.

Test pilots need to know a lot of math. Glenn had never taken some of the math courses other pilots had, such as calculus and trigonometry. He had to work twice as hard as the pilots who had better math backgrounds. Many times he studied until three o'clock in the morning. It was hard work, but he never quit. He graduated from test-pilot school in August 1954.

On July 16, 1957, Glenn took his place in the record books when he broke a cross-country speed record in the Navy's F8U-Crusader jet. He flew from California to New York City in just a little over three hours and twenty-three minutes. That time beat the previous record set by the Air Force by about twenty-three minutes. Glenn was awarded his fifth Distinguished Flying Cross.

In 1958, the National Aeronautics and Space Administration (NASA) was formed. They began the search for their first astronauts. These would be the astronauts for Project Mercury. Project Mercury was the program designed to send the first Americans into space. Glenn wanted to be part of that program.

As an astronaut candidate, Glenn was given every kind of medical test. NASA also needed to know if he could handle the extreme conditions he might encounter in space. They began a series of unusual tests.

Glenn was baked in a heat chamber for two hours at

135°F. His feet were dunked in ice water to see if the shock would raise his blood pressure. He was left sitting alone in a dark, soundproof room for three hours to see if he could stand the isolation of space. Glenn passed all of NASA's tests.

Glenn appears delighted as he stands in front of his F8U-Crusader jet in New York City. He crossed the United States in record speed, beating the previous record set by the Air Force in 1955.

On April 9, 1959, a press conference was held in Washington, D.C. At that conference, America's first seven astronauts were introduced as the Mercury 7. Glenn, who was thirty-seven years old, was the oldest of the group. He was also the only Marine. Earlier, he had received a military promotion. At the press conference he was introduced as Lieutenant Colonel John H. Glenn, Jr.

The astronauts began their training at Langley Air Force Base near Hampton, Virginia. Unlike the other astronauts, Glenn did not move his family to Hampton. He and Annie Glenn agreed that it would be best for him to move into bachelor quarters near the base. That way, he could focus on his training. He spent weekdays at the base and weekends with his family at their home in Arlington, Virginia.

When he was home, Glenn talked to his teenage children about his work. He used a globe, a model of the Mercury capsule, and charts to help them understand exactly what he would be doing.

There was no planned fitness program for the astronauts. It was up to them to keep in shape. Glenn jogged five miles a day to stay fit. He also swam and lifted weights. He spent his time off waterskiing and boating.

The astronauts worked with some strange machines to get ready for spaceflight. One of them was the centrifuge. The centrifuge had a long arm with a closable bucket at one end. An astronaut sat in

Astronauts Scott Carpenter (left) and John Glenn enjoy some time at the beach at Cape Kennedy.

the bucket while the arm swung him in a huge circle as if it were an out-of-control carnival ride. It prepared the astronauts for an increase in g-forces. They would experience this during liftoff and again when they returned to Earth's atmosphere.

The astronauts also helped design the Mercury space capsule. Each of them was assigned to a particular area. Glenn's area was the capsule's control panel.

Only one of the astronauts could make the first flight. It was an honor each of them wanted. "I think that anyone who doesn't *want* to be first doesn't belong in this program," Glenn said.[2]

It was Alan Shepard who became America's first man in space on May 5, 1961. Glenn was disappointed that he had not been chosen for that flight. He felt even worse when he learned he would not get the second flight, either.[3] Virgil Grissom piloted that flight, which took place in July. Glenn served as backup pilot for both of those flights.

Other suborbital flights had been planned, but NASA decided to step up the space program. The next goal was to orbit Earth. John Glenn was selected for that important flight.

The flight was scheduled for December 20, 1961. Unfortunately, it was postponed because of bad weather. Over the next few weeks, the flight was delayed several times because of bad weather or technical problems.

One time, on January 27, 1962, Glenn spent five long hours in the tiny space capsule, waiting to be launched into orbit. After all that time, the flight was postponed again.

The delays were frustrating for everyone involved with the space program, including John Glenn. Each time he climbed into the space capsule, he knew he was risking his life. Time after time he had prepared himself to face that danger, only to have the flight delayed again.

People thought the delays might have a bad effect on Glenn's mental state. However, he was handling the pressure surprisingly well. "I was as disappointed as anyone by the delays," he later wrote, "but they may even have been blessings in disguise . . . I just used the extra time to get more ready."[4]

He worked especially hard learning more about how to use the capsule's manual control system. The space capsule was intended to be flown by an automatic control system. That meant that its flight was controlled by computer. However, there was also a manual control system. With it, the pilot was in control. If anything went wrong with the automatic control system, the pilot would take over. Glenn wanted to be ready.

After much training and some delays, John Glenn was ready to be launched into orbit around Earth in the Mercury space capsule, Friendship 7.

4

A Fireball in the Sky

As a family, the Glenns came up with the name for Glenn's space capsule—*Friendship 7*. The word *friendship* was a reminder that space exploration was done in peace. The number *seven* represented the first seven astronauts.

On February 20, 1962, Annie Glenn and the couple's teenage children gathered in their living room to watch television coverage of the flight. At one end of the room, three television sets had been set up side by side. They were all tuned to different channels. However, at 9:47 A.M., they all showed the same scene—smoke billowing up around the rocket booster as it lifted off the launchpad.

"It is climbing nicely. . . . Pilot John Glenn is reporting all systems go . . . ," a television reporter said.[1]

The rocket soared upward, carrying the space capsule to an exact point in the sky. The capsule had to reach that spot at just the right angle to begin its orbit.

Glenn felt the space capsule shudder. The two outside engines had cut off and dropped away from the rocket. A third engine pushed the capsule higher until the rocket separated from the capsule as planned.

John Glenn was in orbit. He was alone in space inside the small Mercury space capsule. Outside his window,

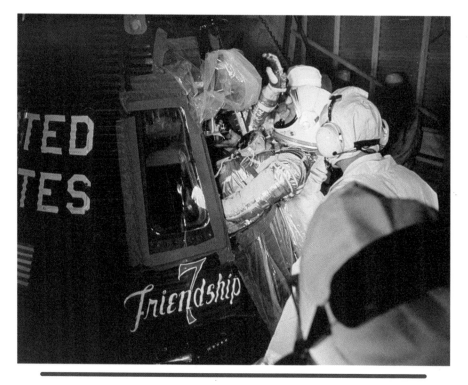

Astronaut John Glenn is helped into the Friendship 7 *capsule.*

the sky was very black. His only contact with Earth was the voices that came to him through his headphones. Speeding through space at over 17,500 miles per hour, Glenn soon lost radio contact with Mission Control. He was out of their range.

Seconds later, he heard another voice. It was the capcom from the Bermuda tracking station. There were eighteen tracking stations set up around the world to monitor Glenn's flight. Some of them were on land. Others were on ships cruising the ocean. Each tracking station had a capcom, or capsule communicator. The capcom was the person who gave Glenn information from Mission Control. Glenn

The Atlas rocket lifts off, blasting the Friendship 7 *capsule and John Glenn into space.*

reported to each capcom as he came into contact with them.

"Starting controls check," Glenn told the Bermuda capcom.[2] He was beginning to check out the capsule's manual control system.

Glenn took photographs of Earth and made observations out the window. "The horizon is a brilliant, a brilliant blue," he said.

Twenty-one minutes after liftoff, he was flying over Africa. "I can see dust storms down there blowing across the desert," he reported.

No American had spent a long period of time in the weightless conditions of space. One of the main things NASA wanted to learn on this flight was how weightlessness would affect an astronaut.

Some doctors thought it might cause dizziness. So far that had not happened to Glenn. In one test, he moved his head up and down, then back and forth, to see if he could make himself dizzy. "The head movements caused no sensations, whatsoever," he reported. "Feel fine."

About forty minutes after liftoff, Glenn saw his first sunset from space. "It went down very rapidly," he said.

It was almost midnight in Australia when Glenn flew over that continent. Looking down from space, he could see a pattern of light. People in the Australian cities of Perth and Rockingham had left their lights on for him.

John Glenn listened to communications from Mission Control while traveling at over 17,500 miles per hour through space.

"The lights show up very well, and thank everybody for turning them on, will you?" Glenn said.

NASA also wanted to know if astronauts would be able to eat in space. It was time to find out. Glenn lifted the visor on his helmet and squeezed applesauce from a tube into his mouth.

Minutes later, he saw his first sunrise in space. He also saw some mysterious specks. "I am in a big mass of some very small particles, that are brilliantly lit up . . . they look like little stars," he noted. No one could figure out what Glenn was seeing.

Near the end of the first orbit, Glenn began having trouble with the capsule's automatic control system. The capsule kept veering off to the side, like a car skidding on ice. The automatic control system corrected this movement each time. However, the corrections were using up too much fuel. It was fuel Glenn would need to reenter Earth's atmosphere. Glenn shut off the automatic control system and began flying the capsule manually to conserve fuel.

At Mission Control, flight controllers had discovered another problem. They were getting a message that the capsule's landing bag was loose. The landing bag was underneath the capsule's heat shield. If the landing bag was loose, then the heat shield must also be loose. If true, this was a serious problem.

The heat shield was Glenn's only protection from the intense heat that would build up around the capsule as it reentered Earth's atmosphere. Without the heat shield, the capsule would burn up in space and Glenn would face a fiery death.

Mission Control decided not to tell Glenn about the problem right away. They put all their energy into finding a way to save Glenn's life.

During the second orbit, Glenn was busy flying the capsule manually. He did not have time to do other work that had been planned for the flight. Glenn was not upset with this change of plans. In fact, he liked it.

Before the flight, some people thought that the

capsules did not need a pilot on board. After all, they had an automatic control system. However, if Glenn had not been on board, Mission Control would have been forced to end the flight when problems began with the automatic control system. Instead, Glenn was able to take control. He actually flew the capsule on this first orbital flight. He proved that pilots were needed in space.

At Mission Control, flight controllers were still trying to figure out what to do about the capsule's heat

The Mission Control Center in Cape Canaveral, Florida, carefully monitored John Glenn's historic trip around Earth. Flight controllers became concerned that the capsule might have difficulties during reentry into Earth's atmosphere.

shield. There was a chance that the message they were receiving was an error.

As Glenn was flying over Australia again, astronaut Gordon Cooper asked him to check on the landing bag. "Will you confirm the landing bag switch is in the off position?" Cooper asked.

"That is affirmative," Glenn answered.

Glenn was cleared for a third orbit. He was getting near the end of that orbit when he flew over the Hawaii tracking station. The Hawaii capcom asked Glenn again to check on the landing bag.

"*Friendship 7*, we have been reading an indication on the ground of segment fifty-one, which is Landing Bag Deploy . . . Cape would like you to check this by putting the landing bag switch in auto position . . . ," the capcom said.

It was a dangerous test. If the landing bag was not already loose, this test could deploy it. Glenn knew that Mission Control had already thought about that, too. They had to have a good reason for asking him to do it. "If that's what they recommend, we'll go ahead and try it," he said.

He flipped the switch to automatic and then back to off. Nothing happened. There was no sign that the landing bag was loose. However, Mission Control was still not certain that the capsule's heat shield was in place.

The heat shield was sandwiched between the

landing bag and the retropackage. The retropackage was made up of three small rockets. The rockets would be fired to slow down the capsule for reentry. Metal straps held the rockets to the outside of the heat shield. After the rockets were fired, the retropackage was to be jettisoned into space.

Mission Control decided to have Glenn leave the retropackage attached during reentry. The metal straps were not strong enough to hold the retropackage on for long. However, they might hold the heat shield in place through the hottest part of reentry.

As Glenn came in contact with the tracking station in California, it was time to fire the retro-rockets. Capcom Wally Schirra told Glenn to leave the retropackage attached until he got to the Texas tracking station. This was a change in plans. Glenn wondered why. He was told that the Texas tracking station would give him that further information.

Glenn felt the capsule jerk when the retro-rockets fired. "It feels like I'm going back toward Hawaii," he said.

However, he was still moving forward, now flying over Texas. "We are recommending that you leave the retropackage on through the entire reentry," the Texas capcom said.

Glenn knew that Mission Control was not telling him everything they knew, and he was not happy about that.[3] "What is the reason for this?" he asked. "Do you have any reason?"

"Not at this time; this is the judgment of Cape Flight," the capcom answered.

Two minutes later, astronaut Alan Shepard at Mission Control explained. "We are not sure whether or not your landing bag has deployed," he told Glenn. "We feel it is possible to reenter with the retropackage on."

Glenn knew that if the heat shield did not do its job, the capsule would burn up in the atmosphere with him inside. There was nothing he could do to prevent it.

Glenn did not have time to think much about that then. He had been flying the capsule manually, conserving fuel so that the automatic control system could take over during reentry. Now that had changed. The automatic control system was not set up to operate with the retropackage attached. Glenn would have to do some of the reentry functions manually.

Mission Control sent one final message. "We recommend that you—"

Glenn did not hear the rest. The capsule was now crashing through Earth's atmosphere. Heat that built up around the capsule set up an electrical field. Radio waves could not travel through it. The blackout had been expected, but it left Glenn alone to face whatever would happen next.

An increase in g-forces felt like a weight on Glenn's

chest as the capsule plunged toward Earth. He heard something smash against the capsule. Then flaming chunks of metal flew past his window. He did not know if it was pieces of the retropackage breaking loose or if it was the heat shield. A bright orange glow built up around the outside of the capsule.

At Mission Control, tension was high. There was nothing anyone could do for John Glenn now. They could only wait, wondering if he was still alive or if he had met a fiery death. The only sound was Alan Shepard's voice as he tried over and over again to reach Glenn by radio. ". . . How do you read?" Shepard asked.

Finally, the radio crackled, and then Shepard heard Glenn's voice. "Loud and clear; how me?" Glenn said.

Everyone at Mission Control began cheering.

"What's your general condition?" Shepard asked. "Are you feeling pretty well?"

"My condition is good, but that was a real fireball, boy," Glenn said. By now, he realized that it was not pieces of the heat shield that he had seen flying past his window. "I had great chunks of that retropack breaking off all the way through," he continued.

Two minutes later, the capsule's large red-and-white parachute opened. It slowed the capsule down even more for its splashdown in the Atlantic Ocean.

Rescuers aboard the destroyer U.S.S. *Noa* saw the parachute. They contacted Glenn by radio, telling him they were on their way.

5

Senator John Glenn

Glenn spent about five hours in space. During that time, he had seen the sun rise and set three times. That evening, he watched one more sunset from U.S.S. *Noa's* deck. Then a helicopter arrived to take Glenn to the aircraft carrier U.S.S. *Randolph*. From there, a Navy jet whisked him off to Grand Turk Island in the Bahamas.

All seven Mercury astronauts gathered at Grand Turk Island. For the next two days, the astronauts, doctors, and NASA officials went over every detail of the flight. They learned that the heat shield on the space capsule had never been loose. The message that Mission Control had received was an error.

Glenn returned to Florida for a hero's welcome. He and his wife, Annie, rode on the back of a white convertible as they made the eighteen-mile trip from the airport to Cape Canaveral. More than one hundred thousand people lined the roadway. They waved and cheered as Glenn rode past. At Cape Canaveral, President John F. Kennedy awarded Glenn the NASA Distinguished Service Medal. The following week, there were parades in Glenn's honor in Washington, D.C.; New York City; and New Concord, Ohio, his hometown.

Astronaut Scott Carpenter became America's fourth man in space and the second to orbit Earth on May 24, 1962. That flight cleared up the mystery of the tiny light particles that Glenn had seen. It turned out that they were caused by human moisture. It came from perspiration and moisture in the astronaut's breath

John Glenn and his wife are joined by Vice President Lyndon B. Johnson during a motorcade ride from the White House to the Capitol building. Glenn's daughter, Lyn, is seated in front of her father.

when he exhaled. The moisture was expelled from the capsule through a vent. Outside the capsule, it froze into tiny ice particles. The particles, which Glenn had seen at dawn, were not visible when the sunlight got brighter.

In 1963, Glenn was assigned to Project Apollo. This was the phase of the space program that would actually land a man on the Moon.

In the meantime, Glenn had become friends with President John F. Kennedy and the president's brother, Robert Kennedy. Newspapers showed photos of the families waterskiing and snow skiing together.

The Kennedys urged Glenn to go into politics. They wanted him to run for the United States Senate seat from Ohio. Glenn said it was too soon after his spaceflight. He did not want to use his popularity as an astronaut to win an election.

That fall, President Kennedy was assassinated. Glenn was deeply affected by Kennedy's death. He began to think that maybe he could serve his country better as a senator. It also appeared that landing on the Moon was several years away. Glenn was already forty-two years old. He knew that he would probably be too old to be considered for a Moon flight.

On January 17, 1964, Glenn announced that he would seek the Democratic Senate seat from Ohio. His opponent was Stephen M. Young, who was already serving in the Senate. Glenn and Young were both Democrats. A political party can nominate only one

At the White House, President John F. Kennedy and John Glenn take a moment to pose for photographers.

candidate for a Senate seat. It meant that the two men would face each other in a primary election. The winner of that election would be the Democratic candidate for the general election in November.

A few weeks later, Glenn was injured when he slipped on a rug in his bathroom. He hit his head on the side of the bathtub, damaging his inner ear. The inner ear is the body's center of balance. Glenn could not move his head without getting dizzy. "Your brain doesn't know where your body is," Glenn's doctor told him. "That's what makes you dizzy."[1]

The dizziness was so bad that he could not walk or even sit up. All he could do was stay in bed and rest. There was no way of knowing when, or if, he would recover. Glenn decided to drop out of the Senate race.

There were rumors that his condition was caused by his spaceflight. Glenn could not figure out why anyone would think that. "I *never* was dizzy for a moment either during my flight or for any time after it," he noted. "Why should I suddenly get dizzy two years later?"[2]

It took several months for Glenn to recover. His illness and his campaign for the Senate had left him in debt. Early in 1965, Glenn retired from the Marines and accepted a position as vice president for Royal Crown Cola. He later bought part-ownership in four motels.

Glenn also stayed active in politics, helping Robert Kennedy with his campaign for president of the United States. In June 1968, Robert Kennedy was killed by an assassin—Sirhan Bishara Sirhan.

A few months later, Glenn resigned from Royal Crown Cola. He announced that he would run for the Senate in 1970. His opponent was businessman Howard Metzenbaum. Glenn lost in the primary election, but it was a close race.

The experience taught Glenn a lot about how to run a political campaign. In 1974, he ran against Metzenbaum again in the primary election. This time, Glenn won. He went on to beat the Republican candidate in the general election and became senator of Ohio.

Glenn was reelected to the Senate in 1980, winning by the biggest margin in the history of Ohio. In 1983, he announced that he would seek the Democratic nomination for president of the United States. He was unsuccessful in that campaign, but he was reelected to the Senate in 1986. In 1992, Glenn became the first United States Senator from Ohio to be elected to four consecutive terms.

Glenn earned a reputation as a hardworking senator.

He was an expert in the areas of technology and science. He worked against the spread of nuclear weapons and tried to put an end to wasteful government spending.

It appeared likely that he would be reelected in 1998. Then, on February 20, 1997, at the age of seventy-five, Glenn announced that he would retire when his current term ended. He said that age was the reason he had decided not to run again.

Glenn had chosen a special place and day to talk about his future. He made the announcement of his retirement from Brown Chapel at Muskingum College in New Concord, Ohio. It came on the thirty-fifth anniversary of his historic spaceflight.

Glenn has had several successful careers: combat pilot, test pilot, astronaut, businessman, and senator. He has always been guided by his desire to serve his country and to do what is right. He is proof that people can achieve their dreams. All it takes is hard work and determination.

John H. Glenn, Jr., served as a United States senator for twenty-four years.

CHRONOLOGY

1921—John Herschel Glenn, Jr., born on July 18 in Cambridge, Ohio.

1939—Graduated from high school; enrolled at Muskingum College in New Concord, Ohio.

1941—Earned his pilot's license; withdrew from college and joined the Navy.

1943—Earned his wings and joined the Marine Corps; married Annie Castor on April 6.

1944—Fought in the Pacific during World War II; flew fifty-nine combat missions.

1945—Son, David, born on December 13.

1947—Daughter, Carolyn (Lyn), born on March 19.

1953—Flew ninety combat missions during the Korean War.

1954—Graduated from Naval Test Pilot School.

1957—Set a cross-country speed record as a test pilot.

1959—Became one of the first seven astronauts.

1962—Became the first American to orbit Earth on February 20.

1964—Made his first bid for a United States Senate seat; was forced to withdraw from the campaign after he was injured in a fall in his bathroom.

1965—Retired from the Marines; began working for Royal Crown Cola.

1974—Elected to the United States Senate.

1980—Elected to a second Senate term.

1983—Sought nomination for president of the United States.

1986—Elected to a third Senate term.

1992—Elected to a fourth Senate term.

1997—Announced that he would not run for a fifth term in the Senate, but would retire when his term ended in 1998.

CHAPTER NOTES

Chapter 1

1. NASA Audio Highlights Tape, "Mission: Project Mercury, 1961-1963," Tape NAA-07, Lion Recording Services.

2. Alan Shepard and Deke Slayton, *Moon Shot: The Inside Story of America's Race to the Moon* (Atlanta: Turner Publishing, Inc., 1994), p. 145.

3. *Results of the First United States Manned Orbital Space Flight* (Washington, D.C.: National Aeronautics and Space Administration, 1962), p. 149.

4. Ibid., p. 150.

5. Ibid.

Chapter 2

1. Paul Healy, "'Mr. America' in the Senate," *Saturday Evening Post,* vol. 247, December 1975, p. 41.

2. *We Seven, by the Astronauts Themselves* (New York: Simon & Schuster, 1962), p. 30.

3. Jhan and June Robbins, "John Glenn: Aftermath of a Bad Year," *Redbook,* vol. 124, January 1965, p. 68.

4. Frank Van Riper, *Glenn: The Astronaut Who Would Be President* (New York: Empire Books, 1983), p. 70.

5. *We Seven, by the Astronauts Themselves,* p. 31.

Chapter 3

1. "Space," *Time,* vol. 79, March 2, 1962, p. 16.

2. *We Seven, by the Astronauts Themselves* (New York: Simon & Schuster, 1962), p. 21.

3. Frank Van Riper, *Glenn: The Astronaut Who Would Be President* (New York: Empire Books, 1983), p. 157.

4. John Glenn, "Minute by Minute Story of the Flight: 'If You're Shook Up, You Shouldn't Be There,'" *Life,* vol. 52, March 9, 1962, p. 25.

Chapter 4

1. Loudon Wainwright, "For Those Who Cared Most, the Long Watch at Home," *Life,* vol. 52, March 2, 1962, p. 31.

2. *Results of the First United States Manned Orbital Space Flight* (Washington, D.C.: National Aeronautics and Space Administration, 1962). All in-flight communications that follow in this chapter come from this source.

3. Frank Van Riper, *Glenn: The Astronaut Who Would Be President* (New York: Empire Books, 1983), p. 174.

Chapter 5

1. Jhan and June Robbins, "John Glenn: Aftermath of a Bad Year," *Redbook,* vol. 124, January 1965, p. 70.

2. Ibid.

GLOSSARY

air-to-air combat—A battle between aircraft in flight.

air-to-ground combat—When an aircraft fires at targets on the ground.

atmosphere—The air surrounding Earth.

backup pilot—A second pilot who trains for a flight along with the pilot who is assigned to the flight. If for some reason the pilot cannot make the flight, the backup pilot takes his place.

capcom—The person who relays information from Mission Control to the flight crew during a space mission and who gets information from the astronauts in flight.

civilian—A citizen who is not part of the nation's military forces.

deploy—To let out or spread out.

Distinguished Flying Cross—Medal awarded to pilots for heroic achievement in flight.

flight controllers—People at Mission Control Center who monitor the flight of a space vehicle.

general election—A vote by a country's citizens to choose among the candidates from different political parties who are running for an office.

jettison—To discard an object to lighten the load of a vehicle.

landing bag—A cushion that opens when a space capsule splashes down in water.

Mission Control Center—A room filled with computers where flight controllers monitor spaceflights.

NASA—National Aeronautics and Space Administration, created in 1958.

orbit—The path of one celestial body or artificial satellite around another.

press conference—A gathering with members of the press present, usually arranged to make an important announcement.

primary election—A vote by members of a political party to nominate a candidate from their party to run for an office.

reentry—The return of an object to Earth's atmostphere, after it has been outside Earth's atmosphere.

retropackage—Three small rockets attached to a space capsule. The rockets are fired to slow down the capsule for reentry. After the rockets are fired, they are jettisoned into space.

scarlet fever—A contagious disease that appears as a red rash on the skin.

suborbital—Making less than one full orbit.

tracking stations—Sites set up by NASA all around the world to monitor the flight of a space vehicle and to help direct the pilot.

zero g—Zero gravity; the absence of gravitational force exerted on a body, causing weightlessness.

FURTHER READING

Cole, Michael D. *Friendship 7: First American in Orbit.* Springfield, N.J.: Enslow Publishers, Inc., 1995.

———. *John Glenn: Astronaut and Senator.* Springfield, N.J.: Enslow Publishers, Inc., 1993.

Hill, Robert W. *What Colonel Glenn Did All Day.* New York: John Day Company, 1962.

Pierce, Lt. Col. Philip N., USMC, and Karl Schuon. *John H. Glenn Astronaut.* New York: Franklin Watts, Inc., 1962.

Van Riper, Frank. *Glenn, the Astronaut Who Would Be President.* New York: Empire Books, 1983.

We Seven, by the Astronauts Themselves. New York: Simon & Schuster, 1962.

INDEX